A Midshipman's Tale

Operation Pedestal

Malta Convoy - August 1942

from the Midshipman's Journal of
Michael MccGwire

Published in 2016 by
Leaping Boy Publications

No part of this book may be reproduced,
stored in a retrieval system or transmitted in any form
by any means without the permission of the publisher.

partners@neallscott.co.uk
www.leapingboy.com

Printed and distributed by Lightning Source UK Ltd.

A CIP catalogue record for this book is available
from the British Library.

ISBN 978-0-9935947-4-8

Contents

The Midshipman	1
Preface	3
Operation Pedestal in Context, Professor Eric Grove	4
Prelude, Michael MccGwire (2008)	7
Instructions for the use of a Midshipman's Journal	8
Narrative, Michael MccGwire (1942)	9
Destroyers which Escort Us	10
August 11th	11
A page from the journal covering 11th-12th August 1942	14
August 12th	15
August 13th	18
Postscript	20

The Midshipman

Michael Kane MccGwire was born in Madras, India (now Chennai) in 1924. His family later returned to the UK and settled in the seaside town of Swanage, Dorset. At thirteen he was sent to the Royal Naval College in Dartmouth. He graduated top of his class, winning the King's Dirk, presented to him by King George VI.

M. K. McCGwire as a Midshipman

In May 1942, aged seventeen, Michael went to sea in the light cruiser HMS *Emerald*; in August he joined the battleship HMS *Rodney* just before it took part in Operation 'Pedestal', the largest Malta Convoy of World War II. Towards the end of the war he was First Lieutenant of the 30th Motor Torpedo Boat Flotilla.

In 1947 the Royal Navy sent Michael to the University of Cambridge for a year to study Russian; his cohort included the later defector George Blake. He then spent a couple of years in Australia, on loan to the Royal Australian Navy, where he met a British occupational therapist, Helen, who was to become his wife. After returning to the UK and working in intelligence in GCHQ, he took his wife and young family to the USSR and was assistant naval attaché at the British Embassy in Moscow.

In 1960 he moved the family to the US for three years, where he was a war-planner at the headquarters of NATO's Supreme Allied Command Atlantic (SACLANT) at Norfolk, Virginia. He returned to the UK and was based in Devonport as the Commander of the submarine depot ship HMS *Adamant*, then transferred to Whitehall to run the Soviet Naval section of the Defence Intelligence Staff. He was the first head of section to speak Russian and to have worked in the USSR. He reshaped the intelligence effort to ask not only how many ships the Soviets had, but to understand what the Soviet Navy was for. It was for his contribution to British naval intelligence that Michael received an OBE in the 1968 New Year Honours list.

Michael retired from the Navy at the age of 42 and took a joint honours degree in Economics and International Politics at the University College of Wales, Aberystwyth. On graduating he became part of the faculty, before going on to become Professor of Maritime and Strategic Studies at Dalhousie University in Canada and then a Senior Fellow at the Brookings Institution in Washington DC, where he wrote *Military Objectives in Soviet Foreign Policy* (1987) and *Perestroika and Soviet Military Policy* (1991).

As a highly respected strategic analyst Michael was best known for the 'MccGwire Thesis' – the idea that the Soviet naval build-up from the 1960s onwards was largely a reaction to the fear of Western maritime superiority, and so could be understood as a defensive posture. He was pleased to be told that this was being taught by the academic staff at his old Alma Mater at Dartmouth. For over 50 years he was also a critic of nuclear deterrence.

Michael wrote up his Midshipman's Tale in 2008. He died in March 2016, aged 91.

Preface

When he was 83, my father Michael MccGwire decided it was time to write up his experiences as a 17-year-old Midshipman in the Second World War. On a shelf in his office was his Midshipman's journal from the time. He set about transcribing his account of what went on during Operation 'Pedestal' when his battleship HMS *Rodney* joined the force that was to protect the convoy ships bound for Malta. He then added notes to explain some of the background and the terms used. He sent a copy by email to each of his of his five children. I read it, printed it out, and put it in a file.

Several years later I came across the Midshipman's Journal itself. It was fascinating to see it written in his handwriting, with comments like 'nothing happened today', the pictures and diagrams he drew and painted when nothing was happening, and the fuzzy photos of one ship taken from another. I came across crossings-out, blotches where a mug had been on the page, the initials of an officer or the Captain and their occasional circle in pencil where he had used inappropriate words or abbreviations (e.g. 'Yankee' instead of 'American'). I tried to imagine my own son and nephews in such a situation at the same age.

So when my father died earlier this year I decided to publish his account of Operation 'Pedestal', with his drawings and photos to illustrate the story. It is remarkable that he was still in possession of his journal over 70 years after he wrote it, under strict wartime rules on secrecy. How he managed to keep it will be explained at the very end.

Lucinda Neall
Leaping Boy Publications
November 2016

Operation Pedestal in Context

Operation 'Pedestal' was one of the major naval operations of the Second World War. So vital did the relief of Malta seem in the summer of 1942 that the rest of the British naval war had effectively to pause in order to concentrate on maintaining the recently decorated George Cross Island. Subsequently there has been debate among historians as to the nature of Malta's strategic importance at this time. Many stress the continued importance of the island as a base for raiding Axis (German and Italian) supply lines across the Mediterranean. Others argue that the island had become a symbol of British imperial power in itself, and the costs of its maintenance outweighed the benefits. Correlli Barnett memorably characterised it as 'the Verdun of the naval war'.

During the years leading up to Operation 'Pedestal' it had proved very difficult to maintain the island as, despite the efforts of Malta-based forces, Rommel's *Panzerarmee Afrika* had advanced in North Africa, creating air bases that made the eastern approach to Malta virtually impossible. If Malta fell it would have been a political disaster for the Churchill administration. The island was the third Imperial bastion that had faced enemy attack. Hong Kong had already fallen; more importantly, so had Singapore. If Malta fell also, Churchill's position, at least as Minister of Defence, if not Prime Minister, might have been fatally undermined. A last convoy sent from the eastern approaches had been forced to turn back.

Such higher political considerations were, at this stage, above the pay grade of a remarkably observant and conscientious Midshipman in one of the two Home Fleet battleships deployed with the most powerful British aircraft carrier force yet seen. We are lucky indeed to have such a first-hand account of this major naval action. Inevitably, such a junior officer could not have been entirely accurate in his wider interpretations, for which he had no first-hand knowledge. Although he did see the old carrier *Eagle* sunk, his hope that the submarine that had torpedoed the ship had itself been sunk was not fulfilled. U73 survived.

Similarly, Midshipman MccGwire's account of the later events reflects his particular location in the unfolding story, but he was able to give us remarkable accurate account. However there is more to be said about the loss of the cruiser *Manchester*. There was no danger of Italian cruiser attack. The Italian fleet had been neutralised by fuel shortage and lack of dedicated air cover. The sad scuttling of HMS *Manchester* was due to a misunderstanding between her commanding officer and her engineering officer about the availability of steam. The cruiser could have tried to escape and drawn fire away from the convoy. Instead the ship was scuttled.

Nevertheless enough ships from Operation 'Pedestal' got through to save Malta – and Churchill's political skin. The engagement also demonstrated a vital new factor in naval warfare, the key importance of carrier-based fighter defence. 'Pedestal' took place at a transitional period when the first lessons of radar-directed fighter control were being put into action. The problem was that available fighter numbers could not deal with the scale of the attack, and *Indomitable* suffered serious damage. She was saved by her armoured hangar protection. Lessons were learned and 'Pedestal' was an important stage in the elevation of the aircraft carrier as the new capital ship, something Midshipman MccGwire noted.

Thanks to 'Pedestal', the tanker *Ohio*'s replenishment of the island's oil (for cooking as well as fuel) and reorganisation of the island's air defences under Air Vice Marshal Sir Keith Park (maintained by the Spitfires from *Furious*) the island held out. Malta was a bastion of Empire that did not fall. However the island was saved in the end by victories in North Africa (rather than vice versa).

We are so lucky to have such a wonderful and perceptive first-hand perspective on this key naval action. I doubt whether any other junior officer could have described things so well.

Professor Eric Grove
Naval Historian

Prelude

Returning from the Indian Ocean, the cruiser *Emerald* called at Devonport to disembark its load of South African bullion and arrived at Portsmouth on 24 July to prepare for docking and refit. On the 29th the five junior Midshipmen were told they had orders to join the battleship *Rodney* at Scapa Flow on 2 August.[1] This allowed a fleeting visit home, before catching the 10.05 train from Euston on 1 August, having spent the previous night travelling or waiting on platforms. They got into Thurso at 7.55, arriving at Scapa Flow aboard the *Dunloose Castle* about 12.30. *Rodney* sent a boat to collect them at 1500 and, as soon as they were aboard, she put to sea, accompanying her sister-ship *Nelson*.

Next morning, the two battleships and their escort joined up with a 14-ship merchant convoy, which had its own escort, which included the cruisers *Nigeria* and *Kenya*. The combined destroyer escort totalled 14 ships, including several 'Tribals', a few 'Hunts', a few 'P's and 'Q's, and the odd 'W' and 'A' class.[2]

Mise en Scene

By July 1942, Malta was running out of food, fuel and ammunition. The American landings in North Africa and the British offensive in Libya were planned for late October/ early November, and it was essential that this strategic lynch-pin should not fall into German hands. As a matter of urgency, the island would have to be re-supplied by sea, requiring a sizeable convoy defended against air, submarine and surface attack, including the threat from Italian battleships and cruisers.

The narrative that follows is an unedited transcript of the writer's Journal.[3] The footnotes may help the reader understand the circumstances aboard ship in 1942, flesh-out some of the technical background, and clarify some of the jargon.

Michael MccGwire, 2008

---

[1] After eleven terms at Dartmouth, the 17-year old cadets went to sea as Midshipmen. In early May 1942, the writer and two of his term-mates were appointed to HMS *Emerald*, a 1920s cruiser stationed in the Indian Ocean.

[2] Different classes of destroyer, dating from the end of WWI to WWII new-construction.

[3] Midshipmen were still 'under training' and beside receiving formal instruction (e.g. celestial navigation) they carried out a range of duties, such as running the ship's boats when in harbour and various kinds of watch-keeping at sea, while their action stations became progressively more demanding (see 16 below). As part of their formal instruction, Midshipmen were required to keep a 'Journal' (S.519) to train them in "the power of observation and expression, and the habit of orderliness". It was inspected regularly and contributed to their final marks on promotion to Sub-Lieutenant. By then, they had spent 18-19 months afloat as Midshipmen, at least 12 of them 'under supervision' aboard a battleship or cruiser, quartered in the 'Gunroom Mess'.

Journal for the use of Midshipmen.

1. The Journal is to be kept during the whole of a Midshipman's sea time. A second volume may be issued if required.

2. The **Officer** detailed to supervise instruction of Midshipmen will see that the Journals are kept in accordance with the instructions hereunder. He will initial the Journals at least once a month, and will see that they are written up from time to time during the month, not only immediately before they are called in for inspection.

3. The **Captain** will have the Journals produced for his inspection from time to time and on a **Midshipman** leaving the ship, and will initial them at each inspection.

4. The following remarks indicate the main lines to be followed in keeping the Journal:—

   (i.) The objects of keeping the Journal are to train Midshipmen in
      (a) the power of observation.
      (b) the power of expression.
      (c) the habit of orderliness.

   (ii.) Midshipmen are to record in their own language their observations about all matters of interest or importance in the work that is carried on, on their stations, in their Fleet, or in their Ship.

   (iii.) They may insert descriptions of places visited and of the people with whom they come in contact, and of harbours, anchorages and fortifications.

   (iv.) They may write notes on fuelling facilities, landing places, abnormal weather, prevailing winds and currents, salvage operations, foreign ships encountered and the manner in which foreign fleets are handled, gunnery and other practices, action in manœuvres, remarks on tactical exercises.
   On the ship making a passage of sufficient interest they should note weather and noon positions.

   (v.) Separate entries need not necessarily be made for each day, full accounts should be given of any event of interest.

   (vi.) The letterpress should be illustrated with plans and sketches pasted into the pages of the Journal, namely:—
      (a) **Track Charts.**
      (b) **Plans of Anchorages** (these should show the berths occupied by the Squadron or Ship, and if a Fleet was anchored the courses steered by the Fleet up to the anchorage).
      (c) **Sketches** of places visited, of coast line, of headlands, of leading marks into harbours, of ships (British or Foreign), of Ports or fittings of ships, or any other object of interest.

5. The Journal is to be produced at the examination in Seamanship for the rank of Lieutenant, when marks to a maximum of 50 will be awarded for it.

Instructions for the use of a Midshipman's Journal

Operation Pedestal, August 1942

<u>Narrative</u>

In the early afternoon of August 7th, *Furious*, *Manchester* and escorting destroyers joined us. *Furious* looked rather gawky with the dovecot perched on one side of her flight deck.[4] We had some warning of her arrival because we had several Albacores flying over us in the morning. That evening *Manchester*, *Eskimo* and *Furious* left us to get ahead into Gibraltar and fuel.

The next day (as we had been warned by the Commander over the public-address system), several aircraft carriers and escorting cruisers joined us. These were *Indomitable* and *Victorious* (two of the latest class aircraft carriers) and *Eagle* and *Furious*, (two of the oldest). Also: *Sirius*, *Phoebe* and *Charybdis*, three *Dido* class cruisers. This addition to our armada was very impressive as, except for two, they were all modern ships and with our two battleships, cruisers and destroyers we were now quite a formidable protection for a convoy of 14 merchant ships.

The disposition of ships on the 8th and 9th was rather complicated as they were always coming and going to refuel or something. After dark on the 9th we steamed through the Straits of Gibraltar, several ships leaving and joining. During the night, fog came down and the whole convoy lost each other, but it cleared and we were able to reform by morning.

We now had a force consisting of:

2 Battleships	4 Aircraft Carriers	7 Cruisers		Destroyers
Nelson*	Eagle	Nigeria*	Charybdis	
Rodney	Furious	Kenya	Phoebe	25-30
	Indomitable	Manchester	Sirius	
	Victorious*	Cairo (AA)		

* Flagships

I don't know exactly how many destroyers we had with us [ie. Force P], but there were 32 engaged in the operation as a whole. That afternoon the Captain spoke and explained what we were to do. The main objective and plan of campaign was as follows. Malta was very short of supplies and the Convoy we were escorting just must get through. It was going to be done as follows:

---

[4] *Furious*, one of the very first carriers in the Royal Navy, used the hull of a WWI-design cruiser, with a flight deck replacing the original superstructure. The 'dovecot' was a purpose-designed bridge structure.

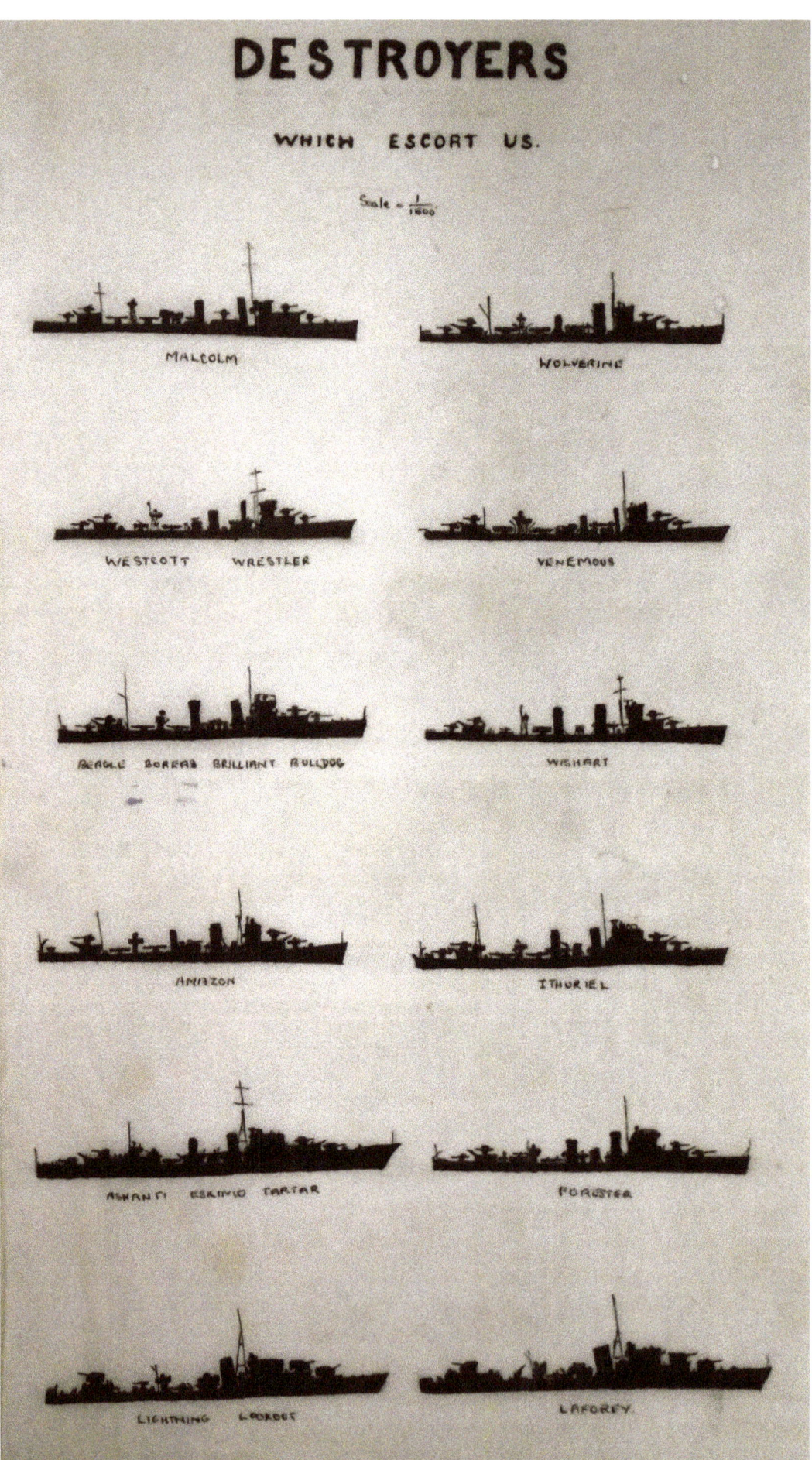

Force P comprised two groups:[5] Force X - the cruisers *Nigeria, Kenya, Manchester, Charybdis, Cairo* and about 10 destroyers; Force Z - *Nelson, Rodney, Victorious, Indomitable, Eagle* and about 10 destroyers, plus cruisers *Sirius* and *Phoebe*. Then there was the Convoy: MS 212, which consisted of 14 merchant ships. There was Force R, made up of two oilers, two tugs (one called *Jaunty*) and odd corvettes and escort vessels; Force Y, which comprised two merchantmen and two destroyers coming the other way; and a small force (*Furious* and about four destroyers) engaged on Operation 'Bellows'.

These forces were to be used as follows. Zero hour was midnight the 9th August; the 10th was Day 1. Force X & Z and the *Furious* were to escort the Convoy. At noon on the Day 2 (Aug 11), *Furious* was to fly off her 24 Spitfires (Operation 'Bellows'), which would go straight to Malta; *Furious* was then to turn back to Gibraltar escorted by 4 destroyers. The rest of us were to rendez-vous Force R and oil our escort made up of 20 destroyers and 7 cruisers. We were then to go on till 1900, Day 3 (Aug 12) when Forces X and Z would split. Force X would turn sharp south and creep through Bomb alley in the night, hugging the Tunisian coast with the Convoy, while we (Force Z) would turn north and try to cause a diversion off the coast of Sardinia to assist Force Y (who would have left Malta on Day 2) in getting through. That's the rough outline. We expected to get attacked first on the evening of Day 2 and continuously on Days 3 & 4.

On Day 1 (Aug 10) nothing happened beyond the usual sub scares and we turned in, wondering on the morrow.

August 11th Today, we knew, we would have our first encounter with the enemy, and for many of us, our first experience of action. But when it came it was so sudden and dramatically unexpected that it quite took our breaths away. After lunch we were all on deck watching *Furious* flying off her Spitfires for Malta. After the last flight had circled, formed up and vanished over the horizon, we settled down to enjoy some of the lovely weather we were having.

Glancing idly round the convoy, I noticed that the *Eagle* was making rather a lot of smoke and was about to add a caustic comment when it seemed to me that she was taking a list to port. And so she was. While we watched she gradually heeled over till her flight deck was awash and then she paused before finally subsiding beneath the sea 4 mins 17 secs after she was hit. The cause of her sinking was two torpedoes which struck on the

---

[5] There were three 'Flagships': *Nelson* - Vice Admiral, in charge of Operation 'Pedestal' and (more immediately) Force Z; *Nigeria* – Rear Admiral, Force X; *Victorious* – Rear Admiral Aircraft Carriers.

port side amidships. She was rather straggling, but the submarine is thought to have dived under the destroyer screen. Over 900 were saved which was miraculous following such a swift sinking. Destroyers shot to the spot and soon depth charges were being dropped. The three *Didos* were steaming up and down the line while the Aircraft Carriers were wheeling astern. The submarine is thought to have been brought to the surface and destroyed.

Soon the tumult died down and the detached escorts rejoined the convoy steaming stolidly on. This event sobered up the ship most noticeably. Beforehand, everyone had been acting as if they were just going on leave, as discipline was relaxed, there was not much work, and there was the general carefree air of a holiday crowd about the ship's company. The sudden loss of *Eagle* made them think twice.

That afternoon we had an alarm and several snoopers [reconnaissance aircraft] were chased from the edge of the convoy. Once, one was shot down.

We went to action stations that evening at about 1800. The first alarm we had was of dive bombers coming out of the sun which turned out to be a snooper chased by 2 of our fighters. Then we got more reports over the P/A system of 'large groups coming in from port or starboard'. Also of several groups which got no further than that, having been intercepted. At about 2050 the first lot of torpedo bombers actually came in. And then all the ships opened up, including us. The noise was positively exhilarating. There was something about the wild rhythm of the pompoms that got in one's blood. Planes were coming in continuously and bombs were being dropped. Two fell close in between us and *Nelson*. Dark was coming now and though we couldn't see very much from the Upper Conning Tower[6], all the ships put up as fine a display of pyrotechnics as I've ever seen on Nov 5th. And then to port there was a burst of flame in the sky and a German bomber crashed to the sea in flames where it burnt for some minutes. There was a temporary lull for about 5 mins at 2112 and then they came in again dropping numerous bombs, several of which were near *Kenya* and merchant ships. We thought we saw two definite torpedo tracks during this action, one passing astern of *Cairo* and one across our bows. Another

---

[6] The detailed nature of this account is explained by the writer's 'action station' as 'Commander's doggy' (personal messenger) during 'Pedestal'. The Commander's action station was in the heavily-armoured 'Upper Conning Tower', located at upper deck level immediately forward of the Octopoidal structure, which housed the ship's bridge (navigational and command), operational plots, and the main armament and high angle directors. As second-in-command of *Rodney,* he had to be able to assume command of the ship, should the Captain and command facilities be disabled. *Rodney's* internal communications system was fairly primitive and vulnerable to action damage; hence the need for personal messengers. If not otherwise engaged, the 'doggy' was required to maintain a detailed log of what was happening. In its raw form, that log was the main source for the Journal's account.

On Malta Convoy – Operation "Pedastal"

salvoes of 8 from her 12 guns & the din was incredible. At 2130 the attack ceased & after remaining closed up for a while we went to cruising station. We had had our first test & it had cost the enemy several planes & no damage to us. Our escorting fighters from the Indomitable & Victorious (Argus had turned back after completion of operation Bellows escorted by several destroyers) found some difficulty in getting back to their ships through our barrage as we weren't all exactly discriminating. It was very interesting listening in to their R/T sets.

On awoke today, realizing that now would come the real test, the incessant attacks one heard of on other convoys. Action Stations at 0515. And then we waited for the expected attack which didn't materialize. The 1st incident of the morning was at 0745 when we did a sudden turn after 2 torpedoes had passed ahead & crossed the tracks of some others. During the morning we were quite often doing these turns as the whole place seems to have been stiff with subs. The aircraft carriers were inspiring sights as they steamed up & down the line on either side flying off & landing aircraft. These fighters were to contribute more to the success of the operation than any other section or units, though followed by the Merchantmen themselves & their destroyers. At 0840 we had an alarm but this turned out to be only a shadower. Then at 0916 we heard "large group of a/c approaching from ahead". We then saw a cloud of smoke come up from the sea as a bomber crashed down. Then quite close on the Stbd bow were some bombs, followed rapidly by 2 Ju 88's among us out of the sun to attack on the other side. 3 sticks fell, one being a very near miss on the Merchant ships to Stbd. The sky was fairly full of aircraft by now.

2nd August 12

A page from the Journal covering 11th - 12th August 1942

plane was down on our port quarter. We put up a tremendous barrage as did the others, the sky being traceried with the tracer from our close range guns. *Manchester* was firing salvos-of-three from her 12 guns and the din was incredible.

At 2130 the attack ceased and, after remaining closed up for a while, we went to cruising stations. We had had our first taste and it had cost the enemy several planes and no damage to us. Our escorting fighters from the *Indomitable* and *Victorious* (*Furious*, escorted by several destroyers, had turned back after completion of Operation 'Bellows') found some difficulty in getting back to their ships through our barrage, as we weren't all exactly discriminating. It was very interesting listening in to their R/T sets.

<u>August 12th</u> We awoke today, realizing that now would come the real blitz, the incessant attacks one heard of on other convoys. Action stations at 0515. And then we waited for the expected attack, which didn't materialise. The first incident on the morning was at 0745 when we did a sudden turn after 2 torpedoes had passed ahead and combed the tracks of some others. During the morning we were quite often doing these turns as the whole place seems to have been stiff with subs. The aircraft carriers were inspiring sights as they steamed up and down the line on either side flying off and landing aircraft. These fighters were to contribute more to the success of the operation than any other sections or units, though followed by the merchantmen themselves and the destroyers. At 0840 we had an alarm but this turned out to be only a shadower. Then, at 0914 we heard "large group of aircraft approaching from ahead". We then saw a cloud of smoke come up from the sea as a bomber crashed down. Then quite close on the starboard bow were some bombs, followed rapidly by two JU88 [dive bombers] coming in out of the sun to attack on the starboard side. Three sticks fell, one being a very near miss on the merchant ship to starboard. The sky was fairly full of aircraft by now. Then at 0925 we saw two black parachutes coming down into the water. These are thought to be the ones used as brakes by dive bombers. After this attack, one dive bomber was sighted diving into the water. There was then a lull. At 0953 we stopped starboard [engine] and turned violently from a suspected torpedo and at 1015 another passed ahead. At 1030 a shadowing aircraft was attacked and was last seen losing height in flames.

From then till about midday nothing much happened except for a few swerves for torpedoes and lots of depth charges were dropped. Then at 1213 four aircraft were approaching. They passed over us and bombs were seen to drop all around the wing destroyer on our port beam. An aircraft was shot down on our port side. This attack was carried out by two formations of high-level bombing SM84s and close bombing by CR2s.

At 1236 what was thought to be a torpedo at the end of its run exploded astern of a destroyer on the starboard wing. Soon after, Manchester opened up, followed by destroyers on the port side as nine torpedo bombers were reported Red 40.[7]

The answer to this was our 16" guns opening up. There was a shattering noise and everyone's vision was obscured by a pall of brown smoke. As soon as this cleared the 16" fired again. When all the smoke had cleared away we couldn't see many signs of planes and of course there are marvellous stories about the effect of our salvos.[8] *However, torpedoes were seen to drop on our port bow and, at about 1246 there were six more torpedo bombers on the port beam. We saw one of them shot down by a fighter on our port bow.*

The starboard side of the convoy was now getting it hot. At 1245 more of these parachutes were seen to come down. The starboard side of the convoy was still quite active beating off torpedo bombers but at 1305 there came a lull, none of the torpedo bombers having been able to get through our destroyer screen. We then had another spasm of dropping depth charges. Then at 1325 more enemy planes appeared on the starboard beam. There was a bomb close astern of Nelson, then three fell across our bows from starboard to just astern of a merchantman on our port bow. More bombs were being dropped, some near misses on merchantmen to starboard and some to port by destroyers. Some close misses on destroyers and more parachutes were dropping. We also saw a plane going into the water.

1323, merchant ship leading the port column seems slightly damaged. 1328, a lull. 1330, damaged merchantman Daqualion is hove to, boats lowered. She is settling by the bow. She has signalled 'I am slightly damaged'. She doesn't look bad and is on a roughly even keel. A destroyer is standing by alongside her. At 1345 an enemy fighter shot across our bows (a Machie 202) after an attempt to drop bombs (almost successfully) on the flight deck of the Victorious. 1350, slight trouble with our No 2 steering motor.

From then till just after 1830, nothing much happed except for a few incidents and continuous dropping of depth charges. Quite a few groups of aircraft were reported approaching but these were always intercepted by

---

[7] On a bearing 40 degrees to port of the ship's heading. Green - starboard.
[8] *Rodney* and *Nelson* were designed and built in the 1920s and their main armament comprised three triple turrets of 16" guns, optimised for surface warfare. This fire power was needed to deter the Italian battleships, but to provide a modicum of anti-air capability the Admiralty had developed a 'time-fuzed' version of the 16" shell, which could contribute to an anti-aircraft 'barrage'. The massive blast of a 16" shell exploding in mid-air (compared to the standard 4.7") could be particularly effective against Italian torpedo bombers that needed to fly straight and low, before dropping their 'fish'.

our fighters. We also prepared to launch our Walrus [flying-boat] to pick up a Fulmar [air] crew, but later didn't as they were so close to land. However, at 1710 a sub was brought to the surface stern first and sank.

1836. Now started the worst and most determined attack we experienced. This was carried out by German-manned Stuka dive-bombers and the difference in the tenacity with which the attacks were pressed home was very noticeable. Everything opened up. At about 1840 two bombs fairly close on port beam and then three just ahead of the *Victorious*. 1842, an armour-piercing bomb came just over X turret and landed in water just off port side and luckily failed to explode.[9] Then just a bit too late they carried out a torpedo-bomber attack with 13 planes from the starboard side. Meanwhile Stukas were diving on the *Indomitable*. I counted eight near misses in one batch, and then another four, and the carrier seemed almost to blow up and became enveloped in smoke. But what impressed us was the way all her guns were firing through this smoke. We heard later that she had two hits forward and one aft, and a small one in the wardroom. She really looked as if she was done for and we were very relieved to see her coming out of the smoke all right with clouds billowing out of the flight deck fore and aft. We saw another plane crash into the water to port.

At 1855 there came a lull, and five minutes later, we saw that *Nelson* had turned about and was steaming away from the convoy, following *Indomitable*, who had hoisted two black balls[10] and did not seem very sure of her steering. We followed *Nelson,* and *Victorious* came too, and we left the convoy steaming on to Malta through the rapidly falling dusk, feeling somewhat ashamed at leaving them in the lurch. *Indomitable's* aircraft were landing on *Victorious* and it made one sad to see them throwing Hurricanes into the water to leave room for other aircraft. I remember noticing a Martlet [fighter] circling *Victorious* until, realising it was hopeless as plane after plane came in ahead of him, the pilot went nose first into the drink. It all seemed so wasteful.

We went on that evening, the four capital ships in line ahead, with *Sirius* and *Phoebe* in company, screened by about nine destroyers.

August 13th And the next day was the same, except at an air raid warning Red, *Victorious* and the rest of us formed up on either side of *Indomitable* and we turned into the wind. Our steering was giving trouble too now,

---

[9] This 'overshot' was a close shave. X Turret was the aftermost 16" turret, immediately forward of the Octopoidal. The fuse on an armour-piercing bomb or shell was activated by the initial impact with the ship's side or upper deck, but fractionally delayed to allow the projectile to penetrate the ship's bowels before exploding.

[10] The international signal for a vessel 'Not under Control'. By this stage, the Italian battleships could no longer pose a threat to the convoy, so (as planned), our capital ships could withdraw.

but we were all making a good 18 knots. On the evening of the 13*th* *Victorious* and *Nelson* turned back to meet the returning cruisers from Force X, and we carried on, arriving in Gibraltar on the evening of the 14*th* escorted by 5 destroyers, one of whom (for instance) had 'spoon' bows after ramming a submarine.

I might as well now tell what happened to the rest of the convoy after we left, from what we learnt in the ship and from the wireless. When we left, the Convoy escort not only lost the four capital ships, but also two cruisers and about 9 destroyers. But the Convoy carried on all right till nightfall, when they were altering the formation of the Force, and then a submarine slipped in and, it is thought, hit with one salvo the *Nigeria* (in the TS)[11], *Cairo* in the screws and the tanker *Ohio*. Anyhow, those three were hit almost simultaneously and Rear Admiral Burrough (Flag Officer, Force X) transferred his flag to the destroyer *Ashanti*, and the cruiser *Nigeria* turned back. *Kenya* also received some damage forward, but carried on. Later on that night, when the Convoy was almost through the [Tunisian] Straits, E-boats attacked and *Manchester* was immobilised and subsequently scuttled, because two Italian cruisers were reported in the vicinity. *Cairo*[12] had also to be sunk and the destroyer *Foresight* went down as well.

However, for all our naval losses,[13] the human casualties were amazingly light. I believe under 400 men, not counting prisoners and wounded. The Convoy went on and ultimately reached Malta the next evening having been attacked continuously by all manner of offensive armament. We had heard previously that the Spitfires had arrived alright, and we are informed that all-in-all 5 of the convoy of 14 got through and on the whole it was a successful operation.[14] But during the night of the 12*th* and on the 13*th* signals were coming in showing the marvellous work going on behind everything by our destroyers. They were towing and towing, and taking off survivors and helping ships. They were really wonderful and the general picture was shown up by messages such as *Penn* v NOIC Malta.[15] "Please tow *Dorset*. Wheat and Petrol essential (repeat) essential to Malta". The struggle that was going on in Bomb Alley to save those ships must have been heroic.

---

[11] TS [Transmitting Station], located below the armoured deck, relatively safe from plunging surface fire, but vulnerable to mines and torpedoes and difficult to escape if the ship were sinking. In the TS, raw data on target range, course and speed provided by the topside 'fire-control' director was converted by the mechanical calculator (the 'fire-control clock') into future target position. This was then transmuted into 'laying' information (elevation and direction) for the guns. Midshipmen were used to 'man' the clock.

[12] *Cairo* was a WWI cruiser that had been converted to a specialised Anti-Aircraft ship.

[13] 1 carrier sunk, 1 badly damaged; 2 cruisers sunk, two damaged; destroyers, numbers lost or damaged unknown at the time of writing.

[14] Four merchant ships got through, relatively unscathed. A fifth, the gallant *Ohio*, a US merchant tanker carrying vital (and highly flammable) aviation fuel, was brought in under-tow by destroyers, its decks awash.

[15] To [destroyer] *Penn* from Naval Officer in Charge, Malta. Please tow …

Postscript

Nelson, Victorious and the cruisers arrived back in Gibraltar during the afternoon of the 16th August, and at 0200 the next morning, *Rodney* and *Victorious* left Gibraltar, bound for UK, where *Rodney* would have its steering fixed in Rosyth. In due course, *Rodney* and *Nelson* would return to the Mediterranean to provide back-up for the Allied landings in North Africa (Operation Torch) at the beginning of November 1942, and cover against the Italian battleships (plus bombardment support) for the invasion of Sicily (Operation Husky) in July 1943.

Midshipmen's exams were held at the end of July,[16] followed by appointments to destroyers for 'small ships' experience, the writer joining *Tyrian* at the beginning of August.[17] Besides working as a Fleet escort during the naval operations supporting the invasion of Italy and the landings at Anzio and Salerno,[18] there were independent operations such as fire-support for army units ashore, routine bombardment, backup for MTBs, anti-E-boat patrols in the Messina Straits, and an interesting few weeks in the Adriatic, based on Bari.

Tyrian was one of the 30 destroyers screening the US battleship *Iowa,* steaming at full speed through the Straits of Gibraltar, bound for the open Atlantic with President Roosevelt aboard, on his way back from the Tehran summit.

By now, *Tyrian* was due for a boiler clean, which meant dry-dock in Gibraltar. This coincided with the arrival of a letter appointing the writer to the Sub-Lieutenants' courses in Portsmouth at the start of 1944, which meant he would be unable to sail with *Tyrian* when she came out of dock.

Rather than hang around waiting for a sea-passage to UK, he reconnoitred the local RAF base and arranged to hitch a ride back (that very evening) in the rear-gunner's turret of a returning Wellington bomber, which happened to be vacant.

---

[16] By this time, the 'senior mids' were fully integrated into *Rodney*'s organisational and operational structure. For example, the writer's 'cruising station' was High-Angle Control Officer (directing the fire of the 4.7" AA guns) and at 'action stations' he was in charge of the High Angle Fire Control Clock (see TS at note 11 above). When the ship was not closed up, he worked in the 'Commander's Office', which was responsible for the production of *Daily Orders* and the routine administration of the ship's company of some 2000 men.

[17] Besides watch-keeping at sea and acting as a general fixer and gofer in harbour, his only regular duty was to provide the obligatory 'Officer' supervision of drawing the rum ration for the ship's company's daily tot: neat for Chief and Petty Officers; cut with two parts water for junior rates (to prevent hoarding).

[18] Which saw the first use of a German 'guided glider bomb' against one of our battleships.

His unscheduled appearance at an RAF Station in Cornwall caused some consternation. Although the Captain of *Tyrian* had approved his sudden departure, the rather unimaginative Station Commander was not convinced and inclined to arrest him for desertion. But it all worked out in the end and, besides the extra leave,[19] yielded an unexpected bonus of retaining his Journal, which would normally have been returned at the end of his Midshipman's training.[20]

---

[19] Six weeks. Previous leave was ten days in August 1942, when *Rodney* was dry docked at Rosyth, on return from 'Pedestal'.

[20] For reasons of wartime security, Midshipmen were required to hand in their Journals on completion of training, lest one should fall into 'enemy hands'. The writer's sudden return to UK meant that this technicality was overlooked, and the journal (along with his other personal effects) was stowed in his 'Service' black-tin-trunk, which was duly forwarded through the Naval Supply system to his home railway station - 'For Collection'. Amazingly, the system worked, although the trunk (clearly marked: MccGwire - Swanage) was 'lost' for several weeks, awaiting collection in Swansea.

If you found A Midshipman's Tale interesting you may also like:

Caroline Davies skilfully incorporates a wealth of material, including recordings and interviews, into a narrative poetry sequence that captures a slice of history in a way that will both inform and move you.

Michael MccGwire, not one to give praise unduly, was very impressed with the work, saying:

> *"I got a better impression of the convoy from that book than from having read reports and being there as a Midshipman. Very evocative – a tour de force!"*

Signed copies available at   advancingpoetry.blogspot.com

Documentary footage of Operation 'Pedestal' can be found on YouTube:
- Operation Pedestal. The Crucial Malta convoy of 1942
- Malta Convoy, The Ohio
- Malta Convoy Battle – British Pathé

Books by Helen MccGwire

The TOM AND JAKE Series

Helen, the English occupational therapist that Michael MccGwire met while he was on loan to the Australian Navy, married him in 1952 and they went on to have five children. They travelled to the Soviet Union and America and on returning to Britain lived in rented farm houses in Devon, Dorset and then Wales. Once the children had left home and Michael and Helen were living in the USA, Helen turned to writing herself, and produced six illustrated children's stories based on the experiences of the family growing up.

Tom and Jake

More About Tom and Jake

Tom and Jake & The Bantams

Tom in the Woods

Tom and Jake & Emily

Tom and Jake & The Storm

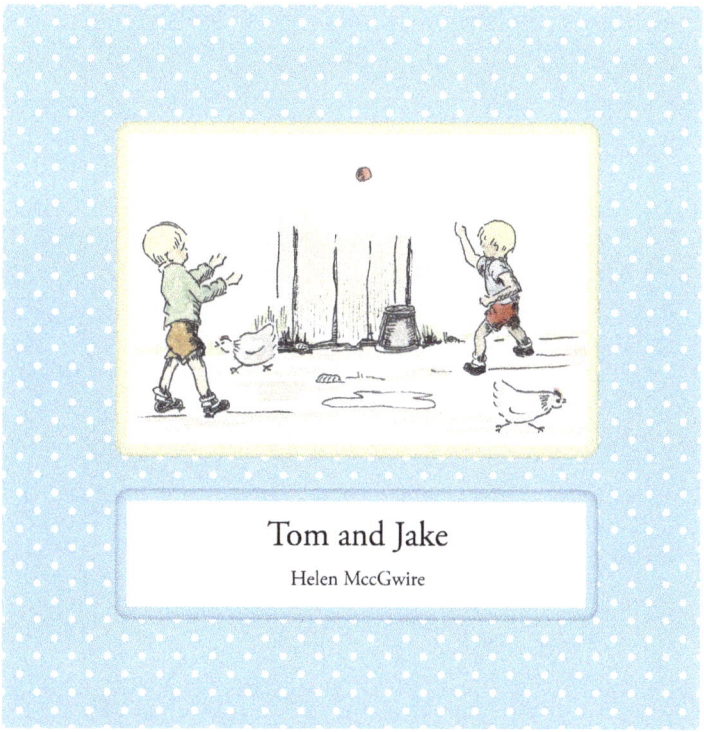

www.leapingboy.com

www.ingramcontent.com/pod-product-compliance
Lightning Source LLC
Chambersburg PA
CBHW041700090426
42744CB00019B/2078